WEEK OF: _______________

THINGS TO DO

Luke's
Gilmore girls™

WEEKLY PLAN

MONDAY	TUESDAY
WEDNESDAY	THURSDAY
FRIDAY	SATURDAY
	SUNDAY

Coffee, please, AND A SHOT OF *cynicism.*

TOP PRIORITIES

DATE	SERVER	GUESTS	CHECK NUMBER

NOTES

THINGS TO DO

Luke's
Gilmore girls™

WEEKLY PLAN

MONDAY	TUESDAY
WEDNESDAY	THURSDAY
FRIDAY	SATURDAY
	SUNDAY

TOP PRIORITIES

DATE	SERVER	GUESTS	CHECK NUMBER

NOTES

Coffee, please, AND A SHOT OF cynicism.

WEEK OF: _______________

Luke's
Gilmore girls™

NO CELL PHONES

WEEKLY PLAN

MONDAY	TUESDAY
WEDNESDAY	THURSDAY
FRIDAY	SATURDAY
	SUNDAY

TOP PRIORITIES

DATE	SERVER	GUESTS	CHECK NUMBER

NOTES

Coffee, please,
AND A SHOT OF
cynicism.

THINGS TO DO

NO CELL PHONES

Luke's
Gilmore girls™

WEEKLY PLAN

MONDAY	TUESDAY
WEDNESDAY	THURSDAY
FRIDAY	SATURDAY
	SUNDAY

Coffee, please, AND A SHOT OF cynicism.

TOP PRIORITIES

DATE	SERVER	GUESTS	CHECK NUMBER

Luke's COFFEE

NOTES

WEEK OF: _______________

THINGS TO DO

NO CELL PHONES

Luke's
Gilmore girls™
WEEKLY PLAN

MONDAY	TUESDAY
WEDNESDAY	THURSDAY
FRIDAY	SATURDAY
	SUNDAY

TOP PRIORITIES

DATE	SERVER	GUESTS	CHECK NUMBER

Luke's COFFEE

NOTES

Coffee, please, AND A SHOT OF *cynicism.*

Luke's

THINGS TO DO

Luke's
Gilmore girls™

WEEKLY PLAN

NO CELL PHONES

TOP PRIORITIES

DATE	SERVER	GUESTS	CHECK NUMBER

MONDAY	TUESDAY
WEDNESDAY	THURSDAY
FRIDAY	SATURDAY
	SUNDAY

NOTES

Coffee, please,
AND A SHOT OF
cynicism.

THINGS TO DO

Luke's
Gilmore girls™

WEEKLY PLAN

NO CELL PHONES

MONDAY	TUESDAY
WEDNESDAY	THURSDAY
FRIDAY	SATURDAY
	SUNDAY

TOP PRIORITIES

DATE	SERVER	GUESTS	CHECK NUMBER

Luke's
COFFEE

NOTES

Coffee, please,
AND A SHOT OF
cynicism.

Luke's

THINGS TO DO

NO CELL PHONES

Luke's
Gilmore girls™
WEEKLY PLAN

MONDAY	TUESDAY
WEDNESDAY	THURSDAY
FRIDAY	SATURDAY
	SUNDAY

TOP PRIORITIES

DATE	SERVER	GUESTS	CHECK NUMBER

NOTES

Luke's COFFEE

Coffee, please,
AND A SHOT OF
cynicism.

Luke's

WEEK OF:

THINGS TO DO

NO CELL PHONES

Luke's
Gilmore girls™

WEEKLY PLAN

MONDAY

TUESDAY

WEDNESDAY

THURSDAY

FRIDAY

SATURDAY

SUNDAY

TOP PRIORITIES

DATE | SERVER | GUESTS | CHECK NUMBER

Luke's
COFFEE

NOTES

Luke's

Coffee, please,
AND A SHOT OF
cynicism.

Luke's

THINGS TO DO

NO CELL PHONES

Luke's
Gilmore girls™

WEEKLY PLAN

MONDAY

TUESDAY

WEDNESDAY

THURSDAY

FRIDAY

SATURDAY

SUNDAY

TOP PRIORITIES

DATE	SERVER	GUESTS	CHECK NUMBER

NOTES

Coffee, please,
AND A SHOT OF
cynicism.

WEEK OF: ______________

THINGS TO DO

Luke's
Gilmore girls™

WEEKLY PLAN

MONDAY	TUESDAY
WEDNESDAY	THURSDAY
FRIDAY	SATURDAY
	SUNDAY

TOP PRIORITIES

DATE	SERVER	GUESTS	CHECK NUMBER

NOTES

Coffee, please,
AND A SHOT OF
cynicism.

THINGS TO DO

Luke's
Gilmore girls™

WEEKLY PLAN

NO CELL PHONES

MONDAY	TUESDAY
WEDNESDAY	THURSDAY
FRIDAY	SATURDAY
	SUNDAY

TOP PRIORITIES

DATE	SERVER	GUESTS	CHECK NUMBER

NOTES

Coffee, please, AND A SHOT OF cynicism.

THINGS TO DO

Luke's
Gilmore girls™

WEEKLY PLAN

TOP PRIORITIES

DATE	SERVER	GUESTS	CHECK NUMBER

MONDAY

TUESDAY

WEDNESDAY

THURSDAY

FRIDAY

SATURDAY

SUNDAY

NOTES

Coffee, please, AND A SHOT OF cynicism.

WEEK OF: ______________

THINGS TO DO

Luke's
Gilmore girls™

WEEKLY PLAN

MONDAY

TUESDAY

WEDNESDAY

THURSDAY

FRIDAY

SATURDAY

SUNDAY

Coffee, please, AND A SHOT OF cynicism.

TOP PRIORITIES

DATE	SERVER	GUESTS	CHECK NUMBER

NOTES

THINGS TO DO

NO CELL PHONES

Luke's
Gilmore girls™

WEEKLY PLAN

| MONDAY | TUESDAY |

| WEDNESDAY | THURSDAY |

| FRIDAY | SATURDAY |

| SUNDAY |

TOP PRIORITIES

DATE	SERVER	GUESTS	CHECK NUMBER

NOTES

Coffee, please, AND A SHOT OF *cynicism.*

WEEK OF: _______________

THINGS TO DO

NO CELL PHONES

Luke's
Gilmore girls™

WEEKLY PLAN

| MONDAY | TUESDAY |

| WEDNESDAY | THURSDAY |

| FRIDAY | SATURDAY |

| | SUNDAY |

Coffee, please,
AND A SHOT OF
cynicism.

TOP PRIORITIES

DATE	SERVER	GUESTS	CHECK NUMBER

NOTES

THINGS TO DO

Luke's
Gilmore girls™

NO CELL PHONES

WEEKLY PLAN

MONDAY	TUESDAY
WEDNESDAY	THURSDAY
FRIDAY	SATURDAY
	SUNDAY

TOP PRIORITIES

DATE	SERVER	GUESTS	CHECK NUMBER

NOTES

Coffee, please,
AND A SHOT OF
cynicism.

THINGS TO DO

Luke's
Gilmore girls™

WEEKLY PLAN

NO CELL PHONES

TOP PRIORITIES

DATE	SERVER	GUESTS	CHECK NUMBER

MONDAY	TUESDAY

WEDNESDAY	THURSDAY

FRIDAY	SATURDAY
	SUNDAY

NOTES

Coffee, please,
AND A SHOT OF
cynicism.

THINGS TO DO

Luke's
Gilmore girls™

NO CELL PHONES

WEEKLY PLAN

MONDAY	TUESDAY
WEDNESDAY	THURSDAY
FRIDAY	SATURDAY
	SUNDAY

TOP PRIORITIES

DATE	SERVER	GUESTS	CHECK NUMBER

NOTES

Coffee, please,
AND A SHOT OF
cynicism.

WEEK OF: ______

THINGS TO DO

Luke's
Gilmore girls™

WEEKLY PLAN

MONDAY	TUESDAY
WEDNESDAY	THURSDAY
FRIDAY	SATURDAY
	SUNDAY

TOP PRIORITIES

DATE	SERVER	GUESTS	CHECK NUMBER

NOTES

Coffee, please, AND A SHOT OF *cynicism.*

WEEK OF: _______________

THINGS TO DO

NO CELL PHONES

Luke's
Gilmore girls™

WEEKLY PLAN

MONDAY	TUESDAY
WEDNESDAY	THURSDAY
FRIDAY	SATURDAY
	SUNDAY

TOP PRIORITIES

DATE	SERVER	GUESTS	CHECK NUMBER

Luke's
COFFEE

NOTES

Coffee, please,
AND A SHOT OF
cynicism.

WEEK OF: ___________

THINGS TO DO

NO CELL PHONES

Luke's
Gilmore girls™

WEEKLY PLAN

MONDAY	TUESDAY
WEDNESDAY	THURSDAY
FRIDAY	SATURDAY
	SUNDAY

Coffee, please, AND A SHOT OF *cynicism.*

TOP PRIORITIES

DATE	SERVER	GUESTS	CHECK NUMBER

NOTES

Luke's COFFEE

Luke's

WEEK OF: _______________

WEEKLY PLAN

MONDAY	TUESDAY
WEDNESDAY	THURSDAY
FRIDAY	SATURDAY
	SUNDAY

TOP PRIORITIES

DATE	SERVER	GUESTS	CHECK NUMBER

NOTES

Coffee, please, AND A SHOT OF cynicism.

WEEK OF: ___________

THINGS TO DO

Luke's
Gilmore girls™

WEEKLY PLAN

MONDAY	TUESDAY
WEDNESDAY	THURSDAY
FRIDAY	SATURDAY
	SUNDAY

TOP PRIORITIES

DATE	SERVER	GUESTS	CHECK NUMBER

NOTES

Coffee, please,
AND A SHOT OF
cynicism.

GILMORE GIRLS and all related characters and elements © & ™ Warner Bros. Entertainment Inc. (s26)

WEEK OF: _______________

THINGS TO DO

NO CELL PHONES

Luke's
Gilmore girls™

WEEKLY PLAN

MONDAY	TUESDAY
WEDNESDAY	THURSDAY
FRIDAY	SATURDAY
	SUNDAY

TOP PRIORITIES

DATE	SERVER	GUESTS	CHECK NUMBER

Luke's COFFEE

NOTES

Coffee, please, AND A SHOT OF *cynicism.*

Luke's

THINGS TO DO

NO CELL PHONES

Luke's
Gilmore girls™

WEEKLY PLAN

MONDAY	TUESDAY
WEDNESDAY	THURSDAY
FRIDAY	SATURDAY
	SUNDAY

TOP PRIORITIES

DATE	SERVER	GUESTS	CHECK NUMBER

Luke's COFFEE

NOTES

Coffee, please,
AND A SHOT OF
cynicism.

Luke's

WEEK OF: ______________

WEEKLY PLAN

MONDAY

TUESDAY

WEDNESDAY

THURSDAY

FRIDAY

SATURDAY

SUNDAY

TOP PRIORITIES

DATE	SERVER	GUESTS	CHECK NUMBER

NOTES

Coffee, please, AND A SHOT OF cynicism.

THINGS TO DO

Luke's
Gilmore girls™

WEEKLY PLAN

MONDAY	TUESDAY
WEDNESDAY	THURSDAY
FRIDAY	SATURDAY
	SUNDAY

TOP PRIORITIES

DATE	SERVER	GUESTS	CHECK NUMBER

NOTES

Coffee, please, AND A SHOT OF cynicism.

WEEK OF:

THINGS TO DO

NO CELL PHONES

Luke's
Gilmore girls

WEEKLY PLAN

TOP PRIORITIES

DATE | SERVER | GUESTS | CHECK NUMBER

MONDAY

TUESDAY

WEDNESDAY

THURSDAY

FRIDAY

SATURDAY

SUNDAY

Luke's
COFFEE

NOTES

Luke's

Coffee, please,
AND A SHOT OF
cynicism.

Luke's

THINGS TO DO

NO CELL PHONES

Luke's
Gilmore girls™

WEEKLY PLAN

TOP PRIORITIES

DATE	SERVER	GUESTS	CHECK NUMBER

MONDAY

TUESDAY

WEDNESDAY

THURSDAY

Luke's COFFEE

NOTES

FRIDAY

SATURDAY

SUNDAY

Coffee, please,
AND A SHOT OF
cynicism.

Luke's

THINGS TO DO

NO CELL PHONES

Luke's
Gilmore girls™

WEEKLY PLAN

MONDAY	TUESDAY
WEDNESDAY	THURSDAY
FRIDAY	SATURDAY
	SUNDAY

Coffee, please, AND A SHOT OF *cynicism.*

TOP PRIORITIES

DATE	SERVER	GUESTS	CHECK NUMBER

NOTES

THINGS TO DO

Luke's
Gilmore girls™

WEEKLY PLAN

NO CELL PHONES

MONDAY	TUESDAY
WEDNESDAY	THURSDAY
FRIDAY	SATURDAY
	SUNDAY

TOP PRIORITIES

DATE	SERVER	GUESTS	CHECK NUMBER

Luke's COFFEE

NOTES

Luke's

Coffee, please,
AND A SHOT OF
cynicism.

THINGS TO DO

NO CELL PHONES

Luke's
Gilmore girls™

WEEKLY PLAN

MONDAY	TUESDAY
WEDNESDAY	THURSDAY
FRIDAY	SATURDAY
	SUNDAY

TOP PRIORITIES

DATE	SERVER	GUESTS	CHECK NUMBER

NOTES

Coffee, please,
AND A SHOT OF
cynicism.

WEEK OF: _______________

THINGS TO DO

Luke's
Gilmore girls™

WEEKLY PLAN

NO CELL PHONES

TOP PRIORITIES

DATE	SERVER	GUESTS	CHECK NUMBER

MONDAY	TUESDAY
WEDNESDAY	THURSDAY
FRIDAY	SATURDAY
	SUNDAY

NOTES

Coffee, please,
AND A SHOT OF
cynicism.

THINGS TO DO

Luke's
Gilmore girls™

WEEKLY PLAN

MONDAY

TUESDAY

WEDNESDAY

THURSDAY

FRIDAY

SATURDAY

SUNDAY

TOP PRIORITIES

DATE	SERVER	GUESTS	CHECK NUMBER

NOTES

Coffee, please,
AND A SHOT OF
cynicism.

WEEK OF: ___________

THINGS TO DO

Luke's
Gilmore girls™

WEEKLY PLAN

MONDAY	TUESDAY
WEDNESDAY	THURSDAY
FRIDAY	SATURDAY
	SUNDAY

TOP PRIORITIES

DATE	SERVER	GUESTS	CHECK NUMBER

NOTES

Coffee, please,
AND A SHOT OF
cynicism.

WEEK OF: ___________

THINGS TO DO

NO CELL PHONES

Luke's
Gilmore girls™

WEEKLY PLAN

MONDAY	TUESDAY
WEDNESDAY	THURSDAY
FRIDAY	SATURDAY
	SUNDAY

Coffee, please, AND A SHOT OF *cynicism.*

TOP PRIORITIES

DATE	SERVER	GUESTS	CHECK NUMBER

NOTES

WEEK OF: _______________

THINGS TO DO

NO CELL PHONES

Luke's
Gilmore girls™

WEEKLY PLAN

| MONDAY | TUESDAY |

| WEDNESDAY | THURSDAY |

| FRIDAY | SATURDAY |

| SUNDAY |

TOP PRIORITIES

DATE	SERVER	GUESTS	CHECK NUMBER

NOTES

Coffee, please, AND A SHOT OF *cynicism.*

THINGS TO DO

WEEKLY PLAN

MONDAY	TUESDAY
WEDNESDAY	THURSDAY
FRIDAY	SATURDAY
	SUNDAY

TOP PRIORITIES

DATE	SERVER	GUESTS	CHECK NUMBER

NOTES

Coffee, please,
AND A SHOT OF
cynicism.